I0570762

Protecting Yourself:
How Data Theft Can Impact You

Privacy Protection Lessons
From a Whistleblower

Danielle Spencer, MIS, MBA, PMP,
FAC-COR III, FAC-P/PM

Disclaimer

The information provided in this book is for general informational and educational purposes only and is not intended as professional advice. While every effort has been made to ensure the accuracy of the information, the content is based on the author's personal experiences and research and should not be used as a substitute for professional guidance, diagnosis, or treatment.

The author and publisher disclaim any responsibility for any adverse effects resulting from the use or application of the information contained in this book. Readers are encouraged to use their own discretion and judgment when applying any advice or recommendations from this book.

The documents and screenshots presented in this book pertain solely to my personal information and records that have been made available to me. These materials do not relate to my employment and are strictly confined to my own experience. No information regarding other individuals or their privacy is included, and no data presented compromises the privacy or experience of anyone else, including any interactions with the Internal Revenue Service (IRS) or other government agencies.

This book is not affiliated with any government agency. The choice to share my personal information is made in an effort to illustrate a potential pattern of abuse by government agencies and the individuals acting within them, possibly related to my role as a whistleblower. It is intended to expose possible misconduct based on my factual, first-hand experiences. The images and documents shown were provided to me by individuals who will remain unnamed and were taken from my personal records.

Any copyrighted materials included in this book that belong to government agencies are used under the doctrine of Fair Use. This use is intended for the purpose of criticism, commentary, and public awareness regarding the actions of these agencies. All content is shared in good faith and within the bounds of legal fair use principles, to support a discussion of governmental practices and potential abuses of power.

The mention of any federal and state government agency in this book is for informational and reference purposes only. The author is not affiliated with, endorsed by, or sponsored by any federal or state agency. Any references to these agencies are based on personal experiences and publicly available information and are not intended to imply official approval, authorization, or endorsement by these agencies.

The information provided about federal agencies and their functions is intended to be accurate and factual at the time of writing. However, readers should independently verify specific details and consult official sources for the most up-to-date information. The use of agency names, terms, or references to government programs does not constitute legal or professional advice, and the author assumes no responsibility for errors, omissions, or changes to the information after publication.

Contents

1. Introduction 1

2. What is Data Theft...3

3. Why does Data Theft Occur 5

    Financial or Material Gain 5

    Knowledge...6

    Blackmail or Extortion.......................................7

    Retribution 8

    Curiosity 9

    Jealousy... 10

4. Potential Impacts of Data Theft.................... 12

5. My Data Theft Experience............................... 16

6. How to Protect Yourself 24

7. Conclusion.. 31

1

Introduction

Tell me if you have had this experience. An employer is vetting you for a job and they ask you and your references questions such as "Do you have any illegitimate children?", "Is there anyone who knows anything embarrassing about you of a sexual nature?" or "What is the financial status of your family; are any of them bribable?"

My guess would be No. Most people haven't. Prior to becoming a whistleblower, that was my response also. Now, my response would be Yes, that happened to me.

My other question is how many of you think that an organization asking and collecting this type of information on potential employees could be a violation of that person's privacy.

If you answered yes, you are correct; it could be a violation of that person's privacy. And this type of privacy violation is called Data Theft.

Hi, I am Danielle Spencer. I am an author, privacy rights and social justice advocate, and an Information Technology (IT) Specialist with almost 25 years of experience. I have a Bachelor's degree in Medical and

Research Technology, two Master's degrees, one in Information Systems and another in Business Administration and have a Master's certification in Information Assurance (Cyber security). I am also project management (PMP) and contract management (FAC-COR III) certified.

Despite all of my credentials and experience, the most important title I have obtained is that of a federal government whistleblower. It was my experience as a whistleblower that taught me about Data Theft. In today's digital society, Data Theft is a real threat to privacy, financial well-being, and even our democracy.

However, Knowledge is Power and being equipped with the knowledge of what Data Theft is, gives you the power. Not only will this book teach you about Data Theft, from my perspective as a whistleblower, but it will also share with you the tactics and techniques I used to both identify and protect myself from its devastating effects.

2

What is Data Theft

Let's start with defining what Data Theft is. Data Theft is a type of privacy violation involving personal or confidential information. I define it as an act of disclosing, communicating, releasing, storing or obtaining personal and/or confidential information without consent **by a person in a trusted position** (e.g. system administrator, office worker, Payroll Specialist, etc.).

The key words in the definition are "by a person in a trusted position." Why are these words key? They are key because they describe a specific type of individual; someone whom we would normally trust. Because these people are in these trusted positions, they are given access to personal and confidential information as part of their job duties. However, access to this information is supposed to be governed by rules and policies. These rules and policies define when these individuals are given permission to access, disclose, or obtain personal and confidential information.

Think about the questions I asked previously, and the scenario in which they were asked. These invasive questions about me and those close to me were asked while I was being vetted for a job. The people doing the vetting were in trusted positions as background investigators. As investigators, they had access to and were allowed to obtain personal information. However, there is and continues to be Office of Personnel Management (OPM) policy that govern background investigation data collection. Based on my research, the act of obtaining and storing information such as the financial status of the family members of a person applying for a job does not fall into any policy guidelines. That is why I believe that Data Theft occurred.

Now that you know what Data Theft is, let's explore the reasons why it can occur.

3

Why does Data Theft Occur

Data Theft can occur for various reasons, not all of which are nefarious or have ill-intent. My experience has taught me that it does occur, and the reasons typically fall into at least one of the following categories: Financial Gain, Knowledge, Blackmail/Extortion, Retribution, Curiosity or Jealously. Let's look at each of them in more detail.

Financial or Material Gain

I believe the most notable and most commonly understood category for people wanting to commit Data Theft is Financial and/or Material Gain. Simply put, this is the act of people debasing their position to get paid. When you think of it in relation to Data Theft, it is a person in a position of trust, committing Data Theft because they want to receive something of value, such as money. For most of us, this is not a hard scenario to imagine. Over the years, there have been several examples of folks selling pictures, medical data, 'stories' or financial data, such as tax returns, to news or tabloid outlets in return for a big payday. Thus, making this a reason why Data Theft occurs that we all can understand.

Knowledge

The second category to define and discuss is Knowledge. Knowledge is information mostly regarded as true or factual. When you think of it in relation to Data Theft, it is a person in a position of trust committing Data Theft to get factual information on a person or company. After I became a whistleblower, I believe that bad actors in the federal government committed Data Theft because they wanted to obtain factual information about me, specifically my personally identifiable information, also known as PII. This included information such as my full name, social security number (SSN), driver's license number, passport number, my current and past addresses, my height, my weight, eye color, where I went to school and current and past employers. It also included identifiable information on my parents, siblings, neighbors, co-workers, supervisors, college professors and friends.

A bad actor, who has this level of FACTUAL detail on a person, can create devastating results for the victim of Data Theft. A bad actor can credibly open credit accounts because they have obtained a SSN, birthday, and address information; an event that typically happens when identity theft has occurred. They could also recreate official documents, such as driver's licenses or Passports, because they have factual information of the data contained on these documents.

Imagine a stalking scenario where the stalker is in a position of trust to commit Data Theft to obtain PII knowledge about the object of their obsession. Or, a person experiencing road rage, who can obtain PII knowledge of a person who they perceived as wronging them on the highway. These are just a few examples where a bad actor can commit Data Theft to obtain factual knowledge on a person.

Blackmail or Extortion

The next category to define and discuss is Blackmail and/or Extortion. Blackmail and Extortion are practices of attempting to force a person or organization into doing a specific course of action so that embarrassing or revealing information is not disclosed. It can include trying to force a person to pay money, but not always. As it relates to Data Theft, this is when a person in a position of trust commits Data Theft because they want to obtain factual information so that they can blackmail or extort a specific entity.

Most well know examples of this occurrence would be when a hacker breaches a company's security defenses, extracts important information (e.g. commits Data Theft), and then threatens to expose this information unless the company either pays a certain amount of money or perform a specific action. There have been public reports of either wealthy people or celebrities, who have been the victims of similar events, by people who either want to receive money or for that person to make public statements.

Retribution

The next category to define and discuss is Retribution. In layman's terms, retribution is the act of exacting revenge or punishment for a perceived wrong. As it relates to Data Theft, a person in a position of trust commits Data Theft because they want to punish a person or a company for a perceived wrong. It is my belief that I experienced Data Theft because there were individuals who wanted to punish me for being a whistleblower.

As I outlined in the second category, a federal government agency obtained my PII and information about people associated with me, without my knowledge, permission or consent, under what I would classify as false pretenses (possible job placement). Having information such as my SSN, passport number, driver's license number and financial information, provides an opportunity for any bad actor to do any number of punishing acts. These acts could include several potential devastating events such as interfering in the tax administration process to cause a person to either have a fraudulent tax debt or to undergo an unnecessary tax audit. This is something that I believed happened to me.

While it is my belief that I was the victim of Data Theft because I am a whistleblower, I believe this can happen in other scenarios to people who are not whistleblowers. This can happen in domestic situations where one person is violent. In this scenario, the violent partner commits Data Theft to punish the non-violent partner either because the non-violent partner contacted law enforcement or moved out of a shared residence.

It can also happen in situations where certain political groups attempt to use ill-gotten information to punish people and organizations who do not comport themselves in a manner that these groups believe is correct.

Curiosity

The next category to define and discuss is Curiosity. Curiosity is a desire to obtain knowledge about a person, company, or situation. As it relates to Data Theft, a person in a position of trust commits Data Theft because they have a curiosity about a person, company or situation. How can curiosity lead to Data Theft? A curious front office staff person working in a doctor's office is one example. See the scenario below.

A doctor's office employee notices a new patient in the waiting room for the fourth day in a row. The worker is curious as to why this patient has been present so often and asks the other office staff. None of them know. Due to the fact that the doctor's office has moved to an electronic record keeping system, office staff no longer input patient data manually. Therefore, unless the staff accesses a patient's electronic medical records, the office staff has no knowledge of a patient's medical status.

On day five, when this employee notices this same patient in the waiting area yet again, his curiosity gets the better of him and he logs into the computer system to review the patient's medical records. The act of reviewing this information, without a business need to know or consent from the patient, violates the organization's policy. Therefore, in this scenario, when this office worker accessed this patient's file to review medical information, because he was curious, he committed Data Theft.

Jealousy

The last category to define and discuss is Jealousy. Many of us understand what jealousy is; it is a feeling of unease or resentment towards another person and/or entity. As it relates to Data Theft, a person in a position of trust commits Data Theft to obtain information about another entity because they are jealous. I can hear the question "How can jealousy lead to Data Theft?" I'll provide this example as a response.

There are two people working in a Human Resources department as Payroll Specialists (Specialists). One of the Specialists, worker A, has been working in the field for many years, much longer than their co-worker. The new co-worker, worker B, has been able to purchase several high-dollar purchases, such as high-end designer handbags and a luxury vehicle. Worker A is a little envious of worker B, because she has always wanted to purchase the items worker B has purchased, seemingly with no problems. Worker A knows the salary range for the Specialist job category. Based on this salary range knowledge, she doesn't believe any Specialist should be able to afford these types of purchases. Worker A wants to know how her co-worker can afford these items.

Instead of asking worker B this question, worker A decides that she can get her question answered by reading the financial information in worker B's personnel file. However, the company policy governing access to personnel files state that files can only be accessed by an employee's supervisor. Worker A is not worker B's supervisor. Moreover, worker A doesn't have a business reason to access and review the personnel file. As such, worker A has just committed Data Theft because she was jealous of the material things worker B possessed.

Now that we know what Data Theft is, and the reasons it can occur, let's talk about some of the potential impacts of Data Theft.

4

Potential Impacts of Data Theft

Whenever someone has their rights infringed upon, it is common to have the feeling of being the victim of abuse. These feelings can range from anger at having your rights violated to embarrassment. In the digital age, where information can be spread quickly, before the Data Theft victim can react, understanding the potential impacts of Data Theft becomes even more necessary. While there are many potential impacts to Data Theft, I will concentrate on the impacts that directly affected me.

Privacy Violation

I believe that the most important impact of Data Theft is that a person's or company's privacy is or has been violated. Why is this important? This is important because Data Theft means that personal, private and/or confidential information is known to people who have no valid business need to know. One potential result of Data Theft is that a person's medical information can be known to people who have no business reason to know. Another potential result of Data Theft is that a person's financial information, to include the amount of money they have in their accounts, if they bounced a check or are encountering financial problems, is known to people without a need to know. These are just a few examples of the type of information that can be learned about people when their privacy has been violated.

In my experience, not only do I believe that my privacy was violated, I believe that the privacy of people associated with me was violated also. When my security file was requested and obtained, without my knowledge or approval, information about family, co-workers, supervisors, and neighbors was obtained also. This information included their full names, current address, phone number and email address. For people related to me, additional identifiable information was obtained to include their date and place of birth.

Companies and other organizations are not exempt from this impact. Data Theft can reveal contract and pricing information to their competitors. It could also provide trade secrets or other confidential and/or trademark information that could either damage the organization's reputation or give a competitor an unfair advantage in the marketplace.

Financial Impact

Another area that could be impacted by Data Theft is a person's or a company's finances. Remember, when Data Theft occurs, the perpetrator obtains FACTUAL information. This information could include a person's SSN, date of birth, and address. This type of information is needed to apply for credit, open bank accounts, or to be seen by a doctor or hospital.

A Data Theft perpetrator could also use this type of information to request fraudulent updates to someone's financial accounts. In the digital age, many transactions occur via an electronic device. A bad actor could credibly request updates to financial accounts because they could use the stolen data to pretend they are the accountholder.

Tax Administration Interference

Interference in the tax administration process is yet another potential impact of Data Theft. This interference can include using Data Theft information to report additional income, report additional deductions, or remove tax documents. As stated previously, when Data Theft occurs, a person's PII can be obtained. A bad actor can use this information to submit false or fraudulent forms to government entities to cause financial harm. This can be a challenge because the Data Theft victim could be liable for a tax bill or be required to undergo a tax audit unfairly. Moreover, on a federal level, this victim may be unable to use the court system to stop this potential impact due to the Tax Anti-Injunction Act.

Fraudulent Document Creation

The final potential impact I want to cover is the creation and distribution of fraudulent documents. In this instance, a bad actor commits Data Theft with the intent of creating a false document using Data Theft information. For most of us, it probably seems improbable that something like this could occur. However, as I stated previously, I'm providing this list of potential impacts based on my experiences as a whistleblower. One of the incidents from my whistleblower experience was when a title search company took judgment and lien information from people not associated with me and used it to create a false title search report. This title search report falsely attributed other people's negative financial data to me and my family in what I believe was a disqualification effort; an effort to say we were not worthy of a certain type of loan.

Due to the ease and confidence with which this company produced this fraudulent report, I began and still do believe that this is a common practice, using invalid information to disqualify people from being able to apply and be approved for credit. While this has the potential to create an issue for people seeking to obtain credit; this can also be an issue for people experiencing financial challenges.

Imagine you are someone who is experiencing financial hardship for any number of reasons – to include being laid off or excessive medical bills. Without your knowledge or consent, a company or bad actor decides to use your financial misfortune as a means to harm another person. In other words, using your financial hardship information to create and distribute documents that detail a low point in your life to disqualify another person – unknown to you. This is why I list this specific category as a potential impact of Data Theft.

To clarify these potential impacts, I'll provide three specific examples of my Data Theft experiences.

5

My Data Theft Experience

During my whistleblower journey, I believe that I was the victim of Data Theft on several occasions. I am sharing these instances because they involve individuals associated with the federal government. I believe this is important because if this type of behavior can be perpetrated by these types of individuals, I believe that it can be perpetrated by employees and associates at other types of organizations.

Obtaining My Security Adjudication File

The first instance I'd like to describe is when the Internal Revenue Service (IRS) requested and obtained my security adjudication file without my knowledge. After becoming a whistleblower, my employment with the IRS ended in October 2017. As such, I did not interview with the IRS for any open positions. Neither had I received any notifications from the IRS that I was being considered for any open IRS positions. Despite this fact, the IRS contacted the Defense Counter-Intelligence Security Agency (DCSA) to obtain my security adjudication file several times in 2018 see screenshot below.

```
(NONE)

CUR 00024 TOT 00047
METHOD    L / LINKAGE    SOI TR02      REQ    DEPARTMENT OF THE TREASURY
PURPOSE   P / PRE-PLACEMENT            ADDR   OFFICE OF SECURITY
DISCLOSED 12/07/2018 ID E321           CITY   WASHINGTON
                                       ST DC        ZIP 20228-0000
MAILED                   ID            CTRY
RETURNED                 ID            NAME

CUR 00025 TOT 00047
METHOD    L / LINKAGE    SOI TR02      REQ    DEPARTMENT OF THE TREASURY
PURPOSE   P / PRE-PLACEMENT            ADDR   OFFICE OF SECURITY
DISCLOSED 12/04/2018 ID E321           CITY   WASHINGTON
                                       ST DC        ZIP 20228-0000
MAILED                   ID            CTRY
RETURNED                 ID            NAME

CUR 00026 TOT 00047
METHOD    L / LINKAGE    SOI TR34      REQ    DEPARTMENT OF THE TREASURY
PURPOSE   P / PRE-PLACEMENT            ADDR   PERSONNEL SECURITY
DISCLOSED 11/19/2018 ID A186           CITY   FLORENCE
                                       ST KY        ZIP 41042-0000
MAILED    11/26/2018 ID 5369           CTRY
RETURNED                 ID            NAME   A186

CUR 00027 TOT 00047
METHOD    L / LINKAGE    SOI TR02      REQ    DEPARTMENT OF THE TREASURY
PURPOSE   P / PRE-PLACEMENT            ADDR   OFFICE OF SECURITY
DISCLOSED 11/06/2018 ID GM50           CITY   WASHINGTON
                                       ST DC        ZIP 20228-0000
MAILED    11/27/2018 ID F851           CTRY
RETURNED                 ID            NAME   TR02

CUR 00028 TOT 00047
METHOD    H / HARDCOPY   SOI TR11      REQ    DEPARTMENT OF THE TREASURY
PURPOSE   P / PRE-PLACEMENT            ADDR   PERSONNEL SECURITY
DISCLOSED 08/15/2018 ID 5185           CITY   FLORENCE
                                       ST KY        ZIP 41042-0000
MAILED    08/15/2018 ID 5185           CTRY
RETURNED                 ID            NAME   SECURITY OFFICE
```

When I inquired with the DCSA as to why this occurred, I was told 'employment purposes', see screenshot below.

Why do I consider this Data Theft? Despite the reasoning and rationale provided by DCSA, I consider this Data Theft because I did not consent for the IRS to have my security file information in 2018. Moreover, I had no knowledge of the agency asking to receive this information, neither was I notified when this information had been provided to IRS. I was a whistleblower against the IRS, which is why my employment ended in 2017. I would not accept employment with that agency given my whistleblower experiences. Therefore, the IRS receiving and obtaining my PII for 'employment' purposes was not and continues to not be plausible to me.

Moreover, if the request for the file was completed in August of 2018, as the DCSA stated, why are there several requests AFTER that date for information? Based on the records provided to me, there are four additional requests for security adjudication file information. As previously stated, I have no records of being contacted by the IRS concerning a potential job opportunity in November or December of 2018.

While I have had this specific experience, the ability for the government to share information without first obtaining consent is concerning to me. For anyone either working for or contracting with the federal government, we provide the government with very detailed, complete and factual information about almost ALL aspects of our lives. This data assembly effort collects information such as your SSN, date of birth, your driver's license number, your Passport number, any and all financial information, every place you have lived for at least the past seven years, the date and times of out of country travel, and identifiable information from relatives (spouse, parents, and siblings), neighbors, friends, co-workers, supervisors, and people who can verify college information (if applicable). Basically, the federal government obtains a 'book of your life'; information that could be used to recreate or imitate anyone – if desired. Due to the amount of factual information compiled in this file, I am extremely cautious of who has this information and desire that the highest security protocols are in place to protect it; not only for myself but for others.

Imagine a scenario where a mentally unstable person can obtain PII on anyone they want by asking. This mentally unstable person doesn't have a valid reason for requesting this type of information or doesn't need to obtain consent to receive it. Moreover, there is No notification requirement, so you aren't aware that someone has obtained your PII. Kinda makes you stop in your tracks, doesn't it? Scenarios like this is why I sincerely believe that Data Theft is a great threat to society. Democracy can become an issue when government actors can obtain your information without your knowledge or consent.

The IRS Verified My Education Information

The second specific incident I'd like to detail is when the IRS contacted a private organization to verify/validate my education credentials - 16 months AFTER my IRS employment ended. In February 2019, for reasons unbeknownst to me, the IRS contacted this company about my education credentials, see screenshot below.

Why do I consider this Data Theft? I consider this Data Theft because I did not consent for the IRS to verify or validate my education credentials. Moreover, since my employment with the agency ended in 2017, I do not believe that the agency had ANY legal or business reason for having this information.

Why do I think this alarming? This is alarming to me because I believe it sets a precedence for organizations or people being able to contact other entities, such as medical or education institutions to verify or validate information on people. Based on my experience, it doesn't appear that the requesting party needed to have a business need or justification for the request. Imagine a scenario where an ex-spouse, an ex-friend, past co-worker, etc. can contact any organization to verify medical, financial, or educational information – without your knowledge or consent. Is it starting to sink-in how Data Theft can negatively impact your life?

Text Message Requesting My PII

The last specific incident that I wanted to detail was a government employee asking for PII via text, see screenshots below. In the text message conversation, I was told that this information was needed so that I could be removed from a government system.

Why do I consider this Data Theft? I consider this incident Data Theft because a person in a position of trust was asking me to provide personal and confidential information using a rationale that I believed was bogus. I also believe that there was an implied threat of retribution if I did not comply with the data request, see screenshot below.

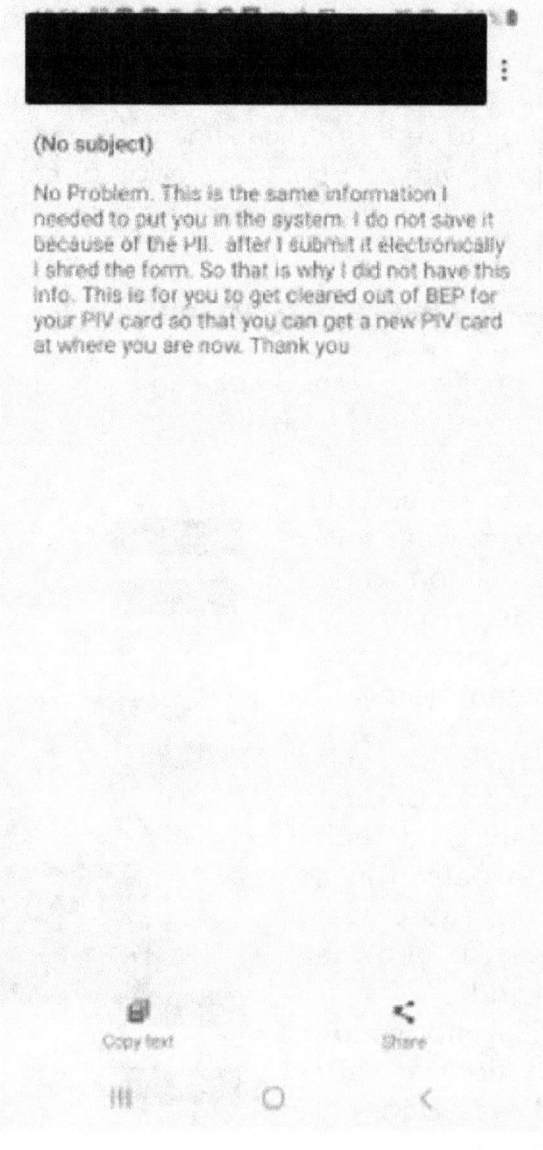

(No subject)

No Problem. This is the same information I needed to put you in the system. I do not save it because of the PII. after I submit it electronically I shred the form. So that is why I did not have this info. This is for you to get cleared out of BEP for your PIV card so that you can get a new PIV card at where you are now. Thank you

Imagine if you were approached by a government official, at the local, state or federal level, in an official capacity, and was asked to provide personal or confidential information. Moreover, after the request was made, there was the hint of an implied threat if you didn't comply. Would this make you believe that your data was safe? My guess would be no.

Now that we know what Data Theft is, the reasons it can occur, the potential impacts of Data Theft, and I have shown you a few examples from my life, let's learn about some practical tactics that we can use to protect ourselves.

6

How to Protect Yourself

Data Theft is a new phenomenon in the digital age. As such, there isn't a 'one size fits all' solution to this new and emerging privacy threat. However, my experience as a whistleblower has taught me a few tactics that can be effective in identifying and combating Data Theft. Provided below are some of the tactics that worked well for me.

1. Know your Rights

The most important thing anyone can do to both protect themselves and to combat Data Theft is to know their rights. As I have stated previously, Knowledge is Power. Many people fall prey to scams and predators because they aren't knowledgeable about their rights. Earlier, I provided an example of questions that I believed violated my privacy (e.g. Data Theft). Unfortunately, at the time of the questioning, neither I nor my references knew the rules or policies governing background investigations. We all assumed that anyone in that position of trust would NEVER exceed their authority to collect information they weren't allowed to collect. Therefore, when we were confronted with these questions, we answered them, even though OPM and other government policy documents did not allow for that type of data collection for the position I was seeking. Had I or my references known this information, we could have handled the situation differently. Since this incident, I have been more diligent in learning my rights, especially as it relates to privacy. I read privacy information for accounts, especially medical and financial accounts. I also ask questions. If a company tells me they need to collect information, I am very comfortable in asking why the information is needed, what it would be used for and how it will be safeguarded.

2. Don't be afraid to say "NO"

Trust me, I know this isn't an easy step for most people, especially if you believe there may be consequences to you saying no. Usually, I have no problem telling people "NO" (especially people not close to me). However, in one of the examples I provided earlier, when I received that text message asking for my PII, I didn't follow what I knew to be true and right. I actually provided my PII to someone via text message. The entire time I was doing it, my gut was telling me that I was making a mistake; especially since I believed the reason for the request was bogus. However, because I was concerned of potential backlash, I provided the requested information.

Don't make the same mistake I did. Most of the time, we know when something just isn't right. We may not be able to put our fingers on why it isn't right, but we have a 'nagging' feeling that it isn't. Listen to that feeling; it could save you a lot of future headaches.

Because I failed to listen to that inner voice, I have NO IDEA how many people or government organizations have my PII now, or which computer systems are storing it.

3. Ask for PII requests in writing, through the postal mail

If you encounter a person or an organization that is persistent that they must have your PII, especially if you think the request is bogus; ask them to send you the request in writing, using postal mail. I do not recommend asking or accepting the request via email or some other carrier service; my suggestion would be to use the United States Postal Service (USPS).

This tactic has two advantages. The first advantage is that if the request is bogus, most likely the requesting party will not send it. My experience has been that few people are willing to go to the extra steps of sending a bogus request via the postal mail.

The second and most important advantage is that if a person or a company is willing to send a bogus request via postal mail, you can request an investigation. Anyone who is bold enough to send a fraudulent request via the postal mail could be liable for committing mail fraud. Mail fraud is considered a felony, a felony that would be investigated by the United States Postal Inspection Service (USPIS). Moreover, the penalties for committing mail fraud could be very consequential.

4. Use Privacy Software

Another tip I suggest is to use various software to protect your privacy. Privacy software goes beyond the use of anti-virus software. It would include using software such as virtual private networks (VPNs) and privacy browsers. I won't suggest a specific type of VPN software or privacy browser; however, I would suggest speaking with a technical specialist, who can tell you which software works best with your electronic devices.

5. Check Accounts Frequently, esp. Financial Accounts

Another tactic that worked very well for me was that I had an established cadence for checking all of my accounts, including my financial and medical accounts. From the age of 18 (I'm over 50 now), every morning, I had a habit of checking every account I had – all of them (I have no idea why I started that habit so long ago). It was a habit I started early in life and one that continues today. However, it was this 'odd' habit that helped me to know when there were potential issues with any of my accounts.

For example, one of the accounts I checked every morning was my credit card. I wanted to ensure that there were no unauthorized charges on my account. One morning, I logged into my account and saw a pending charge for $0.00. Due to the fact that I hadn't used that credit card for some time, I was instantly alarmed. I immediately called the customer service department to obtain more information on the pending transaction. I learned that this pending transaction was generated in a different state. The representative and I agreed that my credit card had been compromised. Therefore, the company was able to cancel the credit card before the pending transaction posted to the account; ensuring that neither myself nor the company lost any money.

Performing the action of checking my account helped me to identify that my credit card had been compromised. Therefore, I would suggest that others have that same practice. Now, I am not suggesting that everyone check all their accounts on a daily basis. However, I am suggesting that everyone find a cadence that works with their schedule, where they check their accounts looking for any questionable transactions.

6. Know who has Accessed Your Records

Another tactic that worked well for me was knowing who had assessed my data records, especially my tax records. Every organization should have a record whenever one of their customer's data records has been accessed. As such, they should be able to provide this information when asked. Knowing who has accessed your data and when goes a far way to being able to tell if and when Data Theft has occurred.

7. Complain, Complain, Complain

When I say this, I mean make your voice heard. If you become the victim of Data Theft, let someone know. It isn't necessary for you to become a national figure (unless you desire to), but, you also shouldn't let the incident go unaddressed. Just like any other criminal activity, when the perpetrator feels like they have gotten away with their bad act, they are emboldened to continue with the bad behavior. The same logic applies to people who commit Data Theft. If people and/or companies feel that they can commit Data Theft with no consequences, they won't stop the behavior. Remember, bad actors thrive in the darkness.

8. Support Privacy and Advocacy Groups

Based on my whistleblower experience, there are very few enforceable laws that support our right to privacy, especially when government officials are involved. Moreover, there are special interest groups who need access to our data to get their agenda implemented. As such, supporting privacy, security, and advocacy groups that fight for our right to privacy helps all of us.

Right now, anyone can go on a state website and get identifying information on people, without a business need to know. For example, in the state of Maryland, I can check the state case database and obtain case information on people, to include their name and address without providing any information about myself. I believe this is problematic because it provides identifying information to anyone who has access to a computer and the internet without asking who is obtaining this information and why. That is why I believe supporting privacy, security and advocacy organizations is important because they can litigate the case of how much personal information should be available in the public sphere.

9. Advocate for Legislative Changes

I listed this one last because I have yet to implement this tactic. However, I do believe this is one that needs to be addressed in the future. During my whistleblower journey, I have learned that this is the one item that has proven to be the hardest obstacle to overcome. This has been true regardless of political party at the local, state and federal level. During my journey, I have seen quite a few situations that I believed would be best resolved by either creating new laws, updating current laws or implementing a policy that imposed fines for perpetrators of Data Theft.

To date, I have yet to obtain any traction. As a matter of fact, when I filed a complaint against the federal government for what I believed was a violation of my Constitutional Right to Privacy (e.g. Data Theft), the case was dismissed. Based on my reading of the matter, I interpreted it to mean that federal government employees could violate my privacy, and I had no recourse because the consequences to me weren't severe enough.

I don't believe that it is acceptable that federal government employees or contractors can violate a person's privacy, and the violated person cannot seek recourse in the civil court system. It is my hope that a majority of Americans don't think so either and will join me in my advocacy efforts to gain more legal protections as it relates to Data Theft.

7

Conclusion

In today's digital world, with almost all of our information being stored, accessed and transmitted electronically, data is a valuable resource. Not only is it valuable to organizations, but it is also valuable to individuals. As such, we as individuals need to understand who is collecting our data, who has access to our data, and how our data is being protected – even by those whose job duties give them access to our data.

My whistleblower journey has opened my eyes to this reality.

If you are interested in learning more about my whistleblower journey:

Checkout out my website at
https://daniellespencer.org/

Connect/Follow me on social media:

LinkedIn:
www.linkedin.com/in/danielle-spencer-20aa6926a

Instagram :
@daniellespencer3647

X :
@DanielleSp43336

YouTube:
@DanielleSpencer-hv5fh

You can also read my Digital Assassins book series, *Digital Assassins: Surviving cyberterrorism and a digital assassination attempt* and *DIGITAL ASSASSINS II: Taking the Whistleblower fight to the Judicial Branch of Government*, on Amazon or Barnes and Noble.